SPOT THE
DIFFERENCE

SPOT THE DIFFERENCE

SEARCH FOR THE CHANGES IN THESE PARALLEL WORLDS

LOUIS CATLETT

SIRIUS

SIRIUS

This edition published in 2023 by Sirius Publishing, a division of
Arcturus Publishing Limited,
26/27 Bickels Yard, 151–153 Bermondsey Street,
London SE1 3HA

ISBN: 978-1-3988-3072-1
AD010843NT

Printed in China

Not everything is as it seems in a parallel universe.

Journey through these surreal scenes and seek
out the changes as you go. At a glance they may
appear identical, but look a little closer and the
differences will begin to reveal themselves.

SEE YOU
ON THE
OTHER SIDE

DIFFERENCES: 20

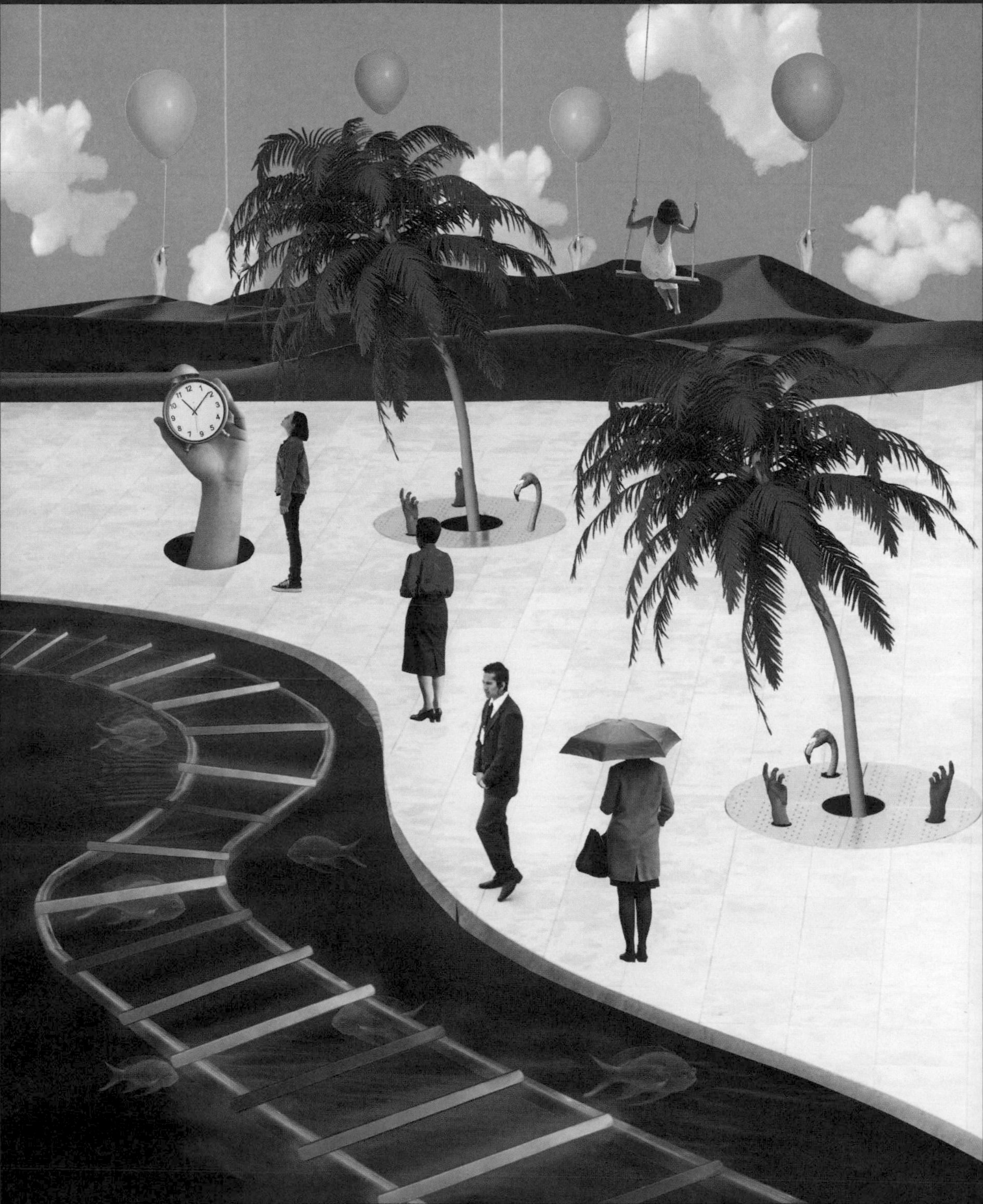

ANSWERS ON PAGE: 88

DIFFERENCES: 15

ANSWERS ON PAGE: 89

DIFFERENCES: 20

DIFFERENCES: 20

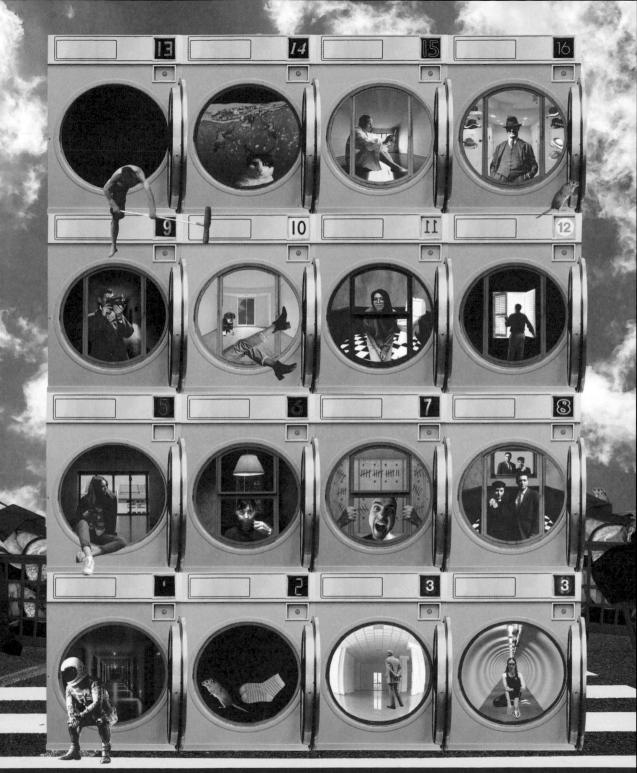

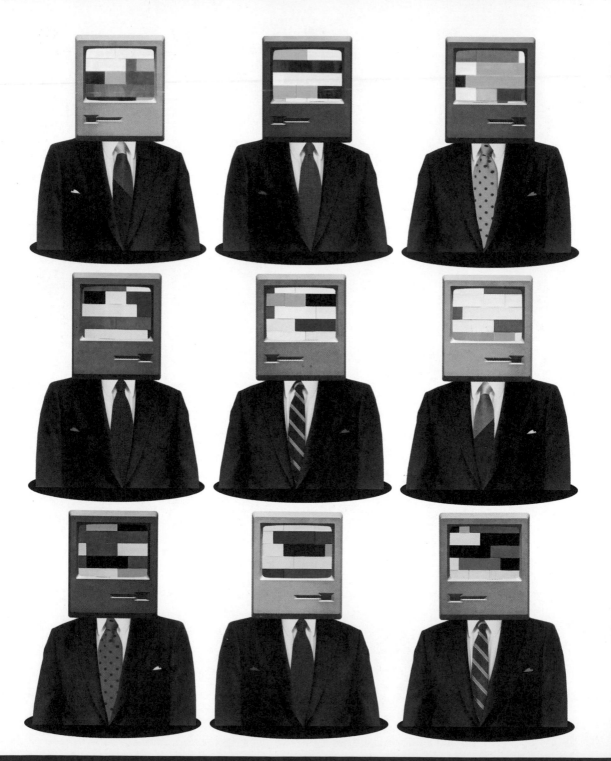

DIFFERENCES: 15

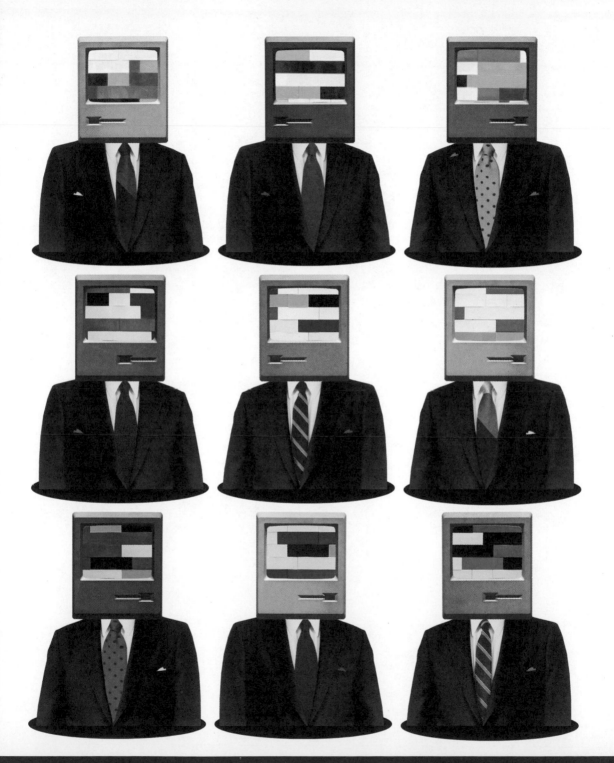

DIFFERENCES: 23

ELEVATC

DIFFERENCES: 16

DIFFERENCES: 20

ANSWERS ON PAGE · 95

DIFFERENCES: 20

DIFFERENCES: 18

DIFFERENCES: 15

ANSWERS ON PAGE: 98

DIFFERENCES: 20

LOOK UP

DIFFERENCES: 21

DIFFERENCES: 20

DIFFERENCES: 14

DIFFERENCES: 20

DIFFERENCES: 14

DIFFERENCES: 18

DIFFERENCES: 20

DIFFERENCES: 20

DIFFERENCES: 19

DIFFERENCES: 17

ANSWERS ON PAGE· 109

DIFFERENCES: 17

DIFFERENCES: 17

ANSWERS ON PAGE · 111

HOT

EXPECT DELAYS

DIFFERENCES: 17

HOT

EXPECT
DELAYS

DIFFERENCES: 21

ANSWERS ON PAGE: 113

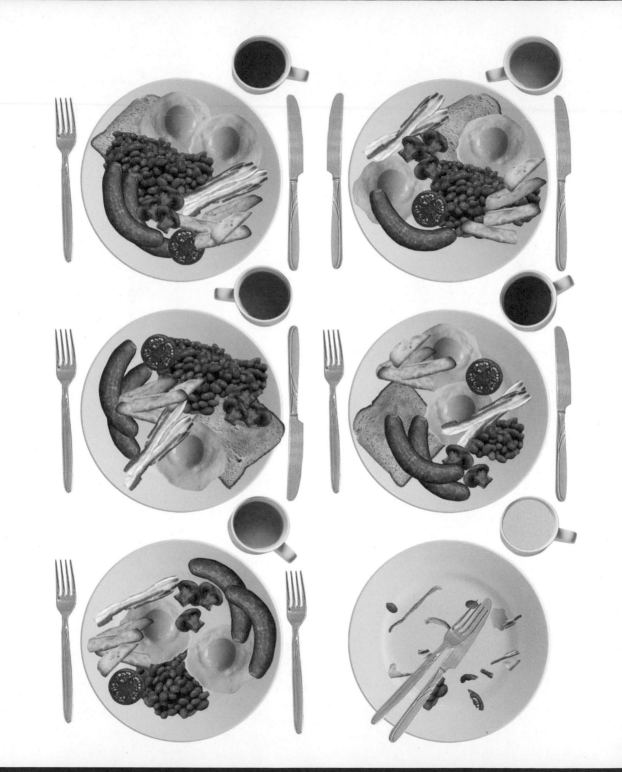

DIFFERENCES: 15

DIFFERENCES: 20

DIFFERENCES: 17

DIFFERENCES: 16

DIFFERENCES: 21

DIFFERENCES: 19

DIFFERENCES: 14

DIFFERENCES: 20

DIFFERENCES: 20

DIFFERENCES: 17

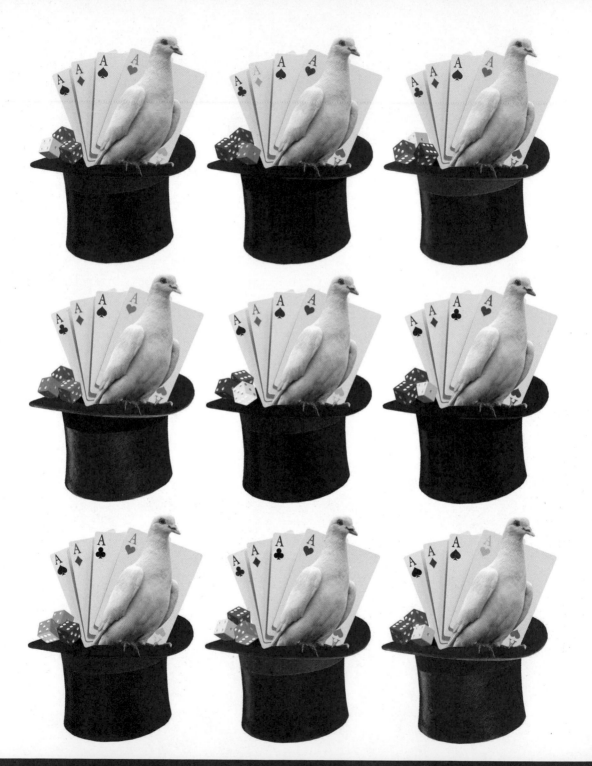

DIFFERENCES: 18

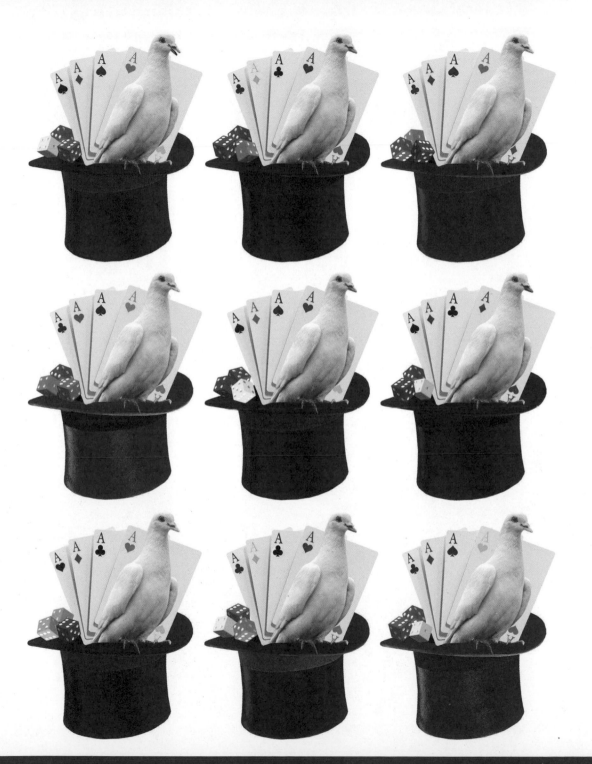

DIFFERENCES: 16

DIFFERENCES: 17

THE EXPERIENCE

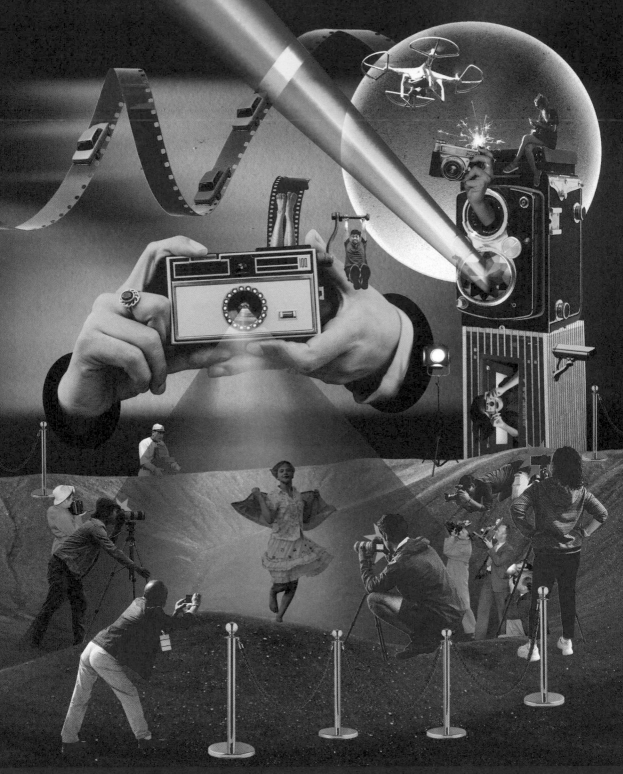

DIFFERENCES: 14

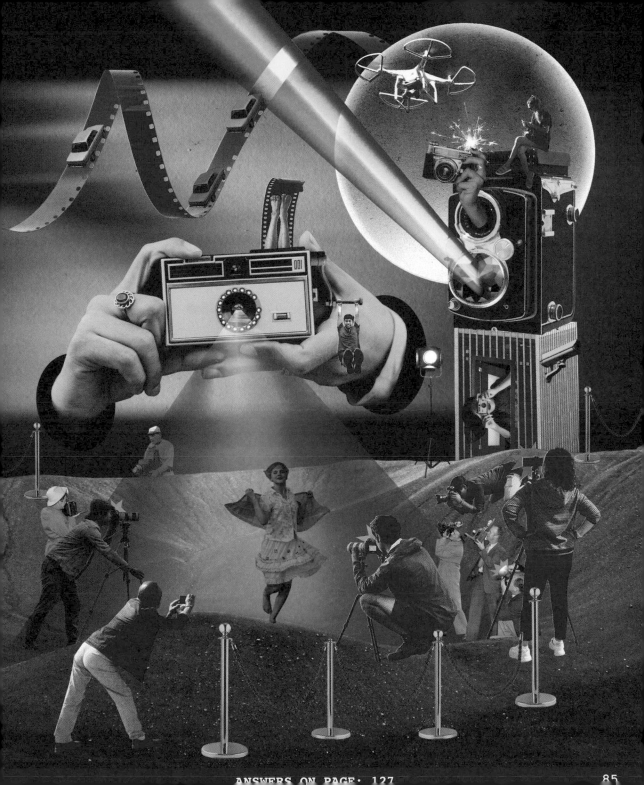

ANSWERS ON PAGE · 127

DIFFERENCES: 20

DIFFERENCES: 15

DIFFERENCES: 16

DIFFERENCES: 20

DIFFERENCES: 15

DIFFERENCES: 21

DIFFERENCES: 20

DIFFERENCES: 14

DIFFERENCES: 14

DIFFERENCES: 20

DIFFERENCES: 19

DIFFERENCES: 17

DIFFERENCES: 17

DIFFERENCES: 15

DIFFERENCES: 17

DIFFERENCES: 16

DIFFERENCES: 21

DIFFERENCES: 14

DIFFERENCES: 20

DIFFERENCES: 18

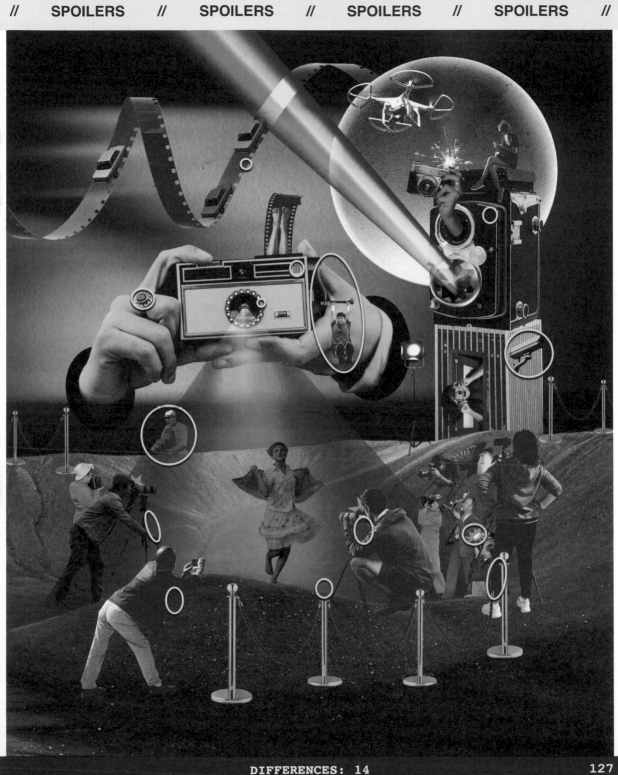

Thanks for taking the time to spot some differences. I hope it provided some enjoyable escapism.

This book is dedicated to my daughter and daily inspiration Dolly.

Thanks to my ever patient partner Anneka, my supportive family and friends.

Thank you Sarah Jennings, Annie Brumsen, Vanessa Daubney and the team at Arcturus Publishing for allowing me the opportunity to create this book.

All artwork has been created using photos from Unsplash and Pixabay. Two invaluable platforms with an incredibly talented community of contributors.